PERFE

LEADER

Terry O'Brien is a best-selling author, columnist, consultant and motivational trainer. He is highly sought-after in the corporate as well as academic world, and has been training managers and providing counselling and consultancy over the past couple of decades. Author of hugely popular books on motivation, effective change and all that is 'un-Google-able', his writings focus on skill development and communication techniques. Terry O'Brien is a firm believer that 'infotainment' is a must for content to be effective, and his books are all about the three 'R's: Read, Record and Recall.

OTHER TITLES IN THE SERIES

Perfect Appraisal

Perfect Assertiveness

Perfect Communication

Perfect CV

Perfect Interview

Perfect Management Skills

Perfect Marketing

Perfect Meeting

Perfect Negotiation

Perfect People Skills

Perfect Personality

Perfect Presentation

Perfect Salesmanship

Perfect Strategy

Perfect Time Management

PERFECT
LEADER

Get it right every time

Terry O'Brien

RUPA

Published by
Rupa Publications India Pvt. Ltd 2017
7/16, Ansari Road, Daryaganj
New Delhi 110002

Sales centres:
Allahabad Bengaluru Chennai
Hyderabad Jaipur Kathmandu
Kolkata Mumbai

ISBN: 978-81-291-4537-6

First impression 2017

10 9 8 7 6 5 4 3 2 1

Typeset by Chetan Sharma

Contents

Introduction   *vii*

1. Leadership: Proactive tools   1

2. Charisma and likeability   5

3. Leadership styles   15

4. Initiatives   30

5. Stepping out of the comfort zone   35

6. Direct action   41

7. Inspiration   52

8. Communication   57

9. Improvisation   67

10. Individuality   75

11. Perseverance   84

12. Leadership: A case study   86

    Bibliography   94

Introduction

Leadership means different things to different people around the world, and different things in different situations. For example, it could relate to community leadership, religious leadership, political leadership and leadership of campaigning groups.

'Leaders are people who do the right thing; managers are people who do things right,' aptly said Professor Warren G. Bennis. Leadership is the art of getting someone else to do something you want done because he wants to do it.

The word 'leadership' can bring to mind a variety of images. For example:

- A political leader, pursuing a passionate, personal cause
- An explorer, cutting a path through the jungle for the rest of his group to follow
- An executive, developing her company's strategy to beat the competition

Leaders help themselves and others to do the right things. They set direction, build an inspiring vision and create something new. Leadership is about mapping out where you need to go to 'win' as a team or an organisation; and is dynamic, exciting and inspiring.

Yet, while leaders set the direction, they must also use management skills to guide their people to the right destination in a smooth and efficient way.

Leaders create an inspiring vision of the future. They motivate and inspire people to engage with that vision. They, in turn, manage delivery of the vision. They coach and build a team, so that it is more effective at achieving the vision. Leadership brings together the skills needed to do these things.

Leadership is the ability to inspire, motivate, energise, engage and move people into action, to move people to accessing their own power to make a change. Leaders can do this because they are respected. To be respected, you must be respectful. Leaders serve as a source of inspiration, courage and clarity; they tend to have a vision of what could be; they tend to have a strong character or personality, which may or may not be charismatic. Leaders tend to be disciplined; they do not abuse their power or authority. Leaders make strategic decisions that will shape conflict.

Leadership: Proactive Tools

Effective leaders provide a rich picture of what the future will look like when their visions have been realised. In business, a vision is realistic. It is the road map of where you want to be in the future. Vision provides direction, sets priorities, and provides a marker. It helps one with a road map so that you can tell that you've achieved what you wanted to achieve.

To create a vision, leaders focus on an organisation's strengths by using these tools.

PEST Analysis

A **PEST** analysis is a business measurement tool. **PEST** is an acronym for *Political, Economic, Social* and *Technological* factors, which are used to assess the market for a business or organisational unit.

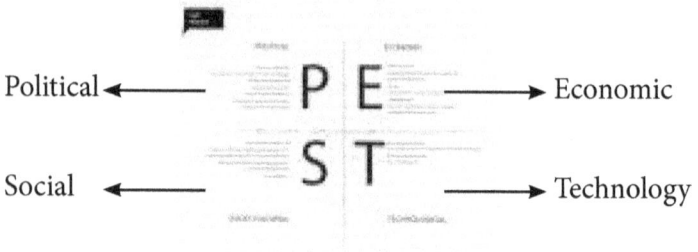

Political ←———— **P** **E** ————→ Economic

Social ←———— **S** **T** ————→ Technology

The basic PEST analysis includes four factors

Political factors are basically how the government intervenes in the economy. Specifically, political factors include tax policy, labour law, environmental law, trade restrictions, tariffs and political stability. Political factors may also include goods and services which the government aims to provide or be provided (merit goods) and those that the government does not want to provide (demerit goods).

Economic factors include economic growth, interest rates, exchange rates and inflation rate. These factors greatly affect how businesses operate and make decisions. For example, interest rates affect a firm's cost of capital and therefore to what extent a business grows and expands. Exchange rates can affect the costs of exporting goods and the supply and price of imported goods in an economy.

Social factors include cultural aspects and health consciousness, population growth rate, age distribution, career attitudes and emphasis on safety. High trends in social factors affect the demand for a company's products and how that company operates.

Technological factors include technological aspects like research and development activity, automation, technology incentives and the rate of technological change. Technological shifts would affect costs and quality, and lead to innovation.

USP Analysis

The Unique Selling Proposition: Finding Your 'Competitive Edge'

Your USP is the unique thing that you can offer that your competitors can't. It's your 'Competitive Edge'. It's the reason why customers buy from you, and you alone.

If you don't have a USP, you're condemned to a struggle for survival—that way lies hard work and little reward.

However, USPs are often extremely difficult to find. And as soon as one company establishes a successful USP in a market, competitors rush to copy it.

Key factors of USP

- Understand the characteristics that customers value
- Rank yourself and your competitors
- Identify where you rank well
- Preserve your USP and use it!

And once you've established a USP, make sure that the market knows about it!

SWOT Analysis

SWOT analysis (alternatively SWOT matrix) is an acronym for *Strengths, Weaknesses, Opportunities* and *Threats*—and is a structured planning method that evaluates these four elements of a project or business venture. A SWOT analysis can be carried out for a company, product, place, industry or a person.

Scenario Analysis

Scenario analysis is a process of analysing possible future events by considering alternative possible outcomes (sometimes called 'alternative worlds'). Thus, the scenario analysis, which is the main method of projection, does not try to show one exact picture of the future.

A compelling vision provides the foundation for leadership. But it's the leader's ability to motivate and inspire people that helps them deliver that vision.

Charisma And Likeability

CHARISMA

There is an assumption that charm and grace are all that is needed to create followers. Of course, self-belief is a fundamental need of leaders. People follow those that they personally admire.

- A charismatic leader gathers followers through dint of personality and charm, rather than any form of external power or authority.

- The feeder to attention: It is interesting to watch a charismatic leader 'working the room' as they move from person to person. They pay much attention to the person they are talking to at any one moment, making that person feel like he or she is, at least for that time, the most important person in the world.

- Charismatic leaders pay a great deal of attention in scanning and reading their environment and are good at picking up the moods and concerns of both individuals and larger audiences. They will then hone their actions and words to suit the situation.

- Charismatic leaders use a wide range of methods to manage their image and if they are not naturally charismatic, they may practise assiduously at developing their skills. They may engender trust through visible self-sacrifice and taking personal risks in the name of their beliefs. They will show great confidence in their followers. They are very persuasive and make very effective use of body language as well as verbal language.

- Deliberate charisma is played out in a theatrical sense, where the leader is 'playing to the house' to create the desired effect. They also make effective use of storytelling, including the use of symbolism and metaphor.

- Many politicians use a charismatic style, as they need to gather a large number of followers. Religious leaders, too, may well use charisma as do cult leaders.

- Charismatic leaders, who are building a group, whether it is a political party, a cult or a business team, will often focus strongly on making the group very clear and distinct, separating it from other groups. They will then build the image of the group, in particular in the minds of their followers, as being far superior to all others.

- Charismatic leaders will typically attach themselves firmly to the identity of the group, such that to join the group is to become one with the leader. In doing so, they create an unchallengeable position for themselves.

- A blend of vision and articulation: Sensitivity to the environment and member needs; personal risk taking; and unconventional behaviour

The truth about effective leaders

- Leaders are made not born.
- You need people around you to be a leader.
- There is no need to be perfect.

However, there is a warning: '*Charisma becomes the undoing of leaders. It makes them inflexible, convinced of their own infallibility, unable to change,*' said Peter Drucker.

The high profile of some leaders is often attributed to a semi-magical quality called charisma. This powerful force seems to allow them to shape events, rather than be shaped by them. Such leaders are personally responsible for what their followers do.

No single characteristic, such as charisma, courage, energy or foresight, entirely explains why people will support a leader.

Some of the most significant chief executives in the history of lively and long-lasting successful companies have not had the personality traits of the typical high-profile, charismatic leader. In fact, many such leaders are virtually unknown outside their own organisation or industry.

Trying to develop charisma as a way of ensuring your leadership is a perfectly natural desire. But it is not a panacea. It will not ensure you become or even stay a leader. You may not need it to lead an organisation successfully.

It is easy to confuse charisma with excellence in other key aspects of leading, such as having a superb vision, being brilliant at getting things done, having a great commitment to developing people. Often great leaders are a product of their organisation, rather than the other way around.

LIKEABILITY

Taking the lead may make you thoroughly unpopular. Leaders are hardly popular figures, even amongst many of their staff. Yet they undoubtedly lead. However, they probably do so despite their abrasive personality or style, rather than because of it. The question whether as a leader it is better to be loved or feared has never been resolved.

The challenges for all of us who lead are:

- Do we lead? Or should we be likeable?
- Can you lead and be likeable?
- What happens if you choose one over the other?

This is a tension that ruins a lot of leadership potential. But it can be managed.

- If you focus on being liked, you won't lead—Leadership requires you to take people to destinations they would not 'go to' or 'reach' without your leadership. Leadership is inherently difficult because it requires a leader to take people where they don't naturally want to go.

You can focus on leading people, or focus on being liked—When you focus on being liked, you will instinctively try to please the people you're leading. And when you do that, you will become confused.

Pleasing people is inherently confusing because some don't agree. One person wants it one way. Another wants it another way. And soon, you're bending over to make everyone happy, which of course means that you will end up making nobody happy, including yourself. It's actually a recipe for misery and inertia. If you focus on being liked, you won't lead. You will never have the courage to do what needs to be done.

- You will have to withstand reasons of being misunderstood—Effective leaders are prepared to be misunderstood. Indeed, there will be seasons in leadership in which you will be misunderstood. Your motives, strategy and skill will be questioned. It will happen to you if you're leading.

There are two extremes that happen when leaders are misunderstood. Some leaders think everyone else is wrong and they're absolutely right. Some leaders believe the critics must be right and question themselves to the point of quitting the change or quitting entirely. We've all seen leaders who are convinced they're right and everyone else is wrong.

So how do you ensure you're not that person without becoming the person who caves in or becomes paralysed in the face of opposition? Simple—Test your motives. Ask yourself: Is this change really going to help people? Or am I doing it for a selfish or questionable reason?

If the change isn't faithful, helpful or going to help people in the long run, abandon it.

If it is honest and it's going to help people in the long run, stick with it.

Leadership is a little like parenting. You do things your kids dislike because it's good for them.

And in leadership, you lead people through seasons they don't want to go through because in the end, it's good for them. And if it's good for them, most of them will thank you in the end. Your job is to get them to the point where they benefit from the change.

Effective leaders are prepared to be misunderstood.

- You can lead and still be likeable—Just because you're leading people to a place they would not naturally go to, doesn't mean you have to abandon grace, humility, kindness, forgiveness or mercy. In fact, the more you embrace characteristics like mercy, kindness, forgiveness, grace and humility, the more effective you will be at leading change. There's a tendency in all of us that longs for the dynamic of 'offer and acceptance'.

I offer you forgiveness, you accept.

I offer you mercy, you say thank you.

I show kindness, you reciprocate.

There will be entire seasons of your leadership in which you will offer all of the above and more and people will not reciprocate.

As a leader, you must be kind when people aren't, even if it hurts. And it will hurt. But in the end, your character will win!

Usually, if the change is a good one and you have led well, people will ultimately see it was a good move. And they will eventually be thankful for it and often to you.

Sometimes—even if the change is good—there will be a few who will never thank you and still won't like you. That's okay, because you took the high road. You can look in the mirror with some satisfaction knowing you did all that you could and did it with all integrity. You fought the good fight.

INTEGRITY

Integrity is one of the top attributes of a great leader. It is based on consistency of actions, values, methods, measures, principles, expectations and outcomes. It connotes a deep commitment to do the right thing for the right reason, regardless of the circumstances. People who live with integrity are incorruptible and incapable of breaking the trust of those who have confided in them. Every human is born with a conscience, the ability to know right from wrong. Choosing the right, regardless of the consequences, is the hallmark of integrity.

Hitler built roads across the nation and ended unemployment; such despots were cruel, charismatic and failed to respect the difference between ends and means. Ultimately such leaders failed.

Leadership can be regarded as amoral, it either exists or it does not. However, leadership that does not contribute to human happiness ultimately fails because of its destructive tendencies. Leadership that contributes constructively to human happiness, earns wide respect. Integrity is what matters.

You will need to discover your own unique way of leading. Merely copying other leaders and their personalities is unlikely to make you sufficiently special to gain real supporters. To discover your special leadership abilities means being willing to keep learning and growing as a human being.

The best leaders know:

- Most leaders are made, not born.

- You can learn to lead.

- You are not a leader in isolation, there must be people willing to be led—supporters.

- Leading means you may be respected, but not necessarily liked.

- You need to discover your own unique way of leading.

- Leaders keep learning and growing.

- Leaders know themselves and what they want.

Practice

Leadership is a verb and productive leadership is an art. The art part is when you use your experience and judgement to apply proven practices to the situation you are in, to produce effective results.

Few leaders always practise great leadership with these qualities.

- Choose action or inaction wisely. Both approaches are appropriate at times.

- Make teamwork a priority. Fix the teamwork issues first and other challenges will be easier to handle.

- Hold planning conversations. The time you spend in up-front conversations will be less than the time you otherwise would spend correcting the unintended consequences of poorly planned and misaligned actions.

- Ensure that the plan is understood. It must have clarity.

- Plan. Look at the products and services you offer today. Which of these will be irrelevant three years from now?

- Create a people strategy. Invest as much in creating the people strategy for your next major change as in developing new processes and systems.

- Learn from success. Looking back, would you say you learned more from your failures than from your successes?

- Stretch the comfort zone. Think about your team's biggest achievement from last year. What have you learned since then, that could have made it bigger? Push your people into the uncomfortable learning zone and coach them to higher levels of success.

- Confirm alignment. Ask each one what he/she plans to do, especially to support each other.

- Get comfortable with silence. Silence can be the prelude to a big decision or decisive action. Use silence in your conversations as thinking and reflecting time.

Practice is how we learn most things and leadership is no different. Be prepared to seek opportunities for practising leadership in as many different settings as possible. Only through practice will you come to lead instinctively, taking on the role effortlessly, almost without thinking.

Practice is one of the most important ways to gain self-confidence as a leader.

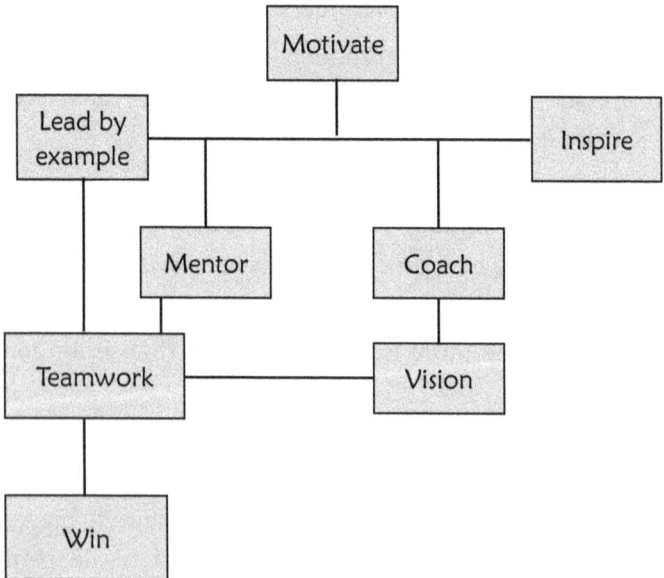

3

Leadership Styles

A leadership style is a leader's style of providing direction, implementing plans and motivating people. There are many different leadership styles that can be exhibited by leaders in the political, business or other fields.

What kind of leadership style should you adopt? Maybe you should be a decisive, autocratic leader who brooks no opposition but gets amazing things done. Or perhaps, you should be a quiet, consultative leader who never makes a move without fully involving everyone.

There is no 'should'. All leaders develop a personal style that is unique to them and you will have to do the same. However, certain trends are making it harder to be one kind of leader as opposed to another and there is also some evidence that having only one style of leadership is too limiting. You need a whole repertoire of styles, which you may adopt for different circumstances.

The way organisations will move in the foreseeable future, it suggests that the old-style 'command and control' leader is no longer so effective. This is because hierarchy is giving way to the idea of a 'community' of shared interests and stakeholders.

New-style leadership is facilitative; it is about empowering relationships with those that might support a leader. In fact, the relationship is mutually supportive, rather than dependent and subordinate. In productive work, effective leaders are not commanders and controllers, bosses and big shots. They are servers and supporters, partners and providers.

This newer form of leadership style unfolds much more energy, talent and commitment.

Leadership is more important than commanding and controlling.

THE SEVEN 'I'S

These are the seven basic principles of leadership.

- Insight
- Initiative
- Inspiration
- Involvement
- Improvisation
- Individuality
- Implementation

The seven 'I's highlight perhaps the most powerful part of effective leadership: the ability to see what is needed.

One has to practise the art of seeing, of discovering what those who would be led need 'at this moment'.

The seven 'I's of Leadership make one look within. They are based on the canons of self-awareness, understanding others and not just 'looking' but 'seeing' the situation.

INSIGHT

Don't look, see! Don't hear, listen!

Leadership insights are an ever more important part of developing as a leader. Leadership is increasingly needed in unpredictable circumstances. Leaders are those who are expected to show the way forward, often by thinking differently. That means you need to stretch your thinking and enhance your practice by applying fresh leadership insights to the workplace. Theories and models are helpful but they can also be a limitation. Insights can provoke you to think differently and suggest practical ways to turn thoughts into action.

There is no shortage of useful and helpful leadership theories and models. Yet sometimes, we need to be encouraged to think differently to:

- provoke our thinking with fresh insight.
- stretch our understanding.
- ignite ideas.

Theories and models can provide useful frameworks for our thinking, but they can also be limiting.

Note: If we allow our thinking to stay within the confines of a framework, this can be counter-productive. Insights which provoke you to think differently about leadership can be a powerful complementary approach to other methods for understanding leadership.

Often it is only with hindsight that we realise the signs were all around us.

Insight is your ability to accurately see events, circumstances and people, and making sense of them. Leaders are strong on insight. Although this can seem a mysterious quality, in essence most people can learn how to develop it.

Insight uses both sides of your brain. There is the part that thinks logically and another part that is more intuitive. We tend to use one at the expense of the other. If you are primarily a logical, systematic person, you can practise tapping into the part of your brain that relies on instinct, feeling and emotion.

If you tend to rely heavily on your intuitive sense of what to do next, you can learn to take advantage of your brain's analytical powers. Even if you are mainly instinctive, your brain still has an extraordinary ability to classify and break down information into smaller, more manageable chunks.

People, events and circumstances often appear chaotic or meaningless.

This ability to interpret, stems from developing your:

- self-awareness,

- understanding of others, and

- perception.

SELF–AWARENESS

Know thyself!

Self-awareness is essential to leadership. It helps you get better, because you know how well you are currently doing. It helps you take the right decisions, because you know your blind spots. It helps you do great work, because you remember past mistakes and address them. Being self-aware is the key to understanding.

Deliberately or otherwise, successful leaders develop considerable personal insight. Often they may not share this with anyone. Yet they are usually aware of what is happening in themselves and how it affects their outward behaviour. If you despise the idea of increasing your self-awareness, then perhaps you should reconsider whether you truly want to be a leader.

Self-awareness is about how you see yourself, about understanding your personality, your strengths and weaknesses. It is also about knowing the difference between how you see yourself and how others see you.

For example, people sometimes imagine that their accent or appearance is holding them back from attaining their potential as a leader. They tend to cling to this belief even though people around them may give them completely contradictory feedback: 'We love your accent'; 'We think you look like a leader'. A negative self-image is destructive and can hold you back.

Genuine self-awareness comes gradually, rather than suddenly like a flash of a light. Occasionally though, one might suddenly gain an entirely new perspective on the world. Self-aware people:

- keep looking at what they do and how they do it.
- know that their leadership is always on the line. They regularly check how they are performing.

You become more self-aware by consciously exploring your:
- driving force,
- current feelings,
- present attitudes, and

- how others around you are feeling and reacting.

Self-awareness is different from being self-conscious. When you are highly self-conscious, it is hard to absorb anything that is not just about you, rather than other people. It stops you from seeing what is happening around you.

Increase your self-awareness by:
- being willing to accept new information about yourself.
- analysing your impact on people around you.

Where would you find such information? You have to deliberately go looking for it. It means you ask for feedback, seek people's opinions and enquire about what they are thinking, maybe put yourself in uncomfortable situations to obtain the information you need.

Checking It Out

There are innumerable ways to explore yourself and who you are. The method matters less than the willingness to discover more about yourself. Many people, though, shy away from any form of self-examination, any type of introspection. Such people seldom make good leaders.

Try developing a clearer picture of your own strengths and weaknesses by creating a sort of personal balance sheet. You can use this to explore how best to develop further and become a more complete person.

Psychometric tests, or personality profiles, are also ways of gaining a new perspective on oneself. These may have many different purposes, for example, to clarify your preferred role in a team, your tendency to take instant action or time to reflect, whether you care more about people or things, whether you are an introvert or an extrovert, how you prefer to learn, and so on.

Self-aware people possess a natural curiosity about themselves. They keep asking questions.

- Why did I do that?
- What effect did I have?
- Why did that work?
- How could I do that better?
- What went wrong with what I did?
- How can I do it again?
- How did they react to what I said or did?
- How am I feeling right now?

UNDERSTANDING OTHERS

You can apply similar methods to gain more understanding of other people. Again, it is less the method you use that is important than your willingness to harness your natural curiosity, your determination to discover more.

With a team, for example, you might regularly speak to people to find out how they are feeling, what they are thinking and what concerns them. More formally, you could ask everyone to complete a series of questionnaires that reveal their personal preferences and other information.

One of the best ways of really understanding others though, is through people-watching — consciously observing them in all kinds of different situations, observing how they behave, rather than just taking their words and actions for granted.

When you understand, others you are not necessarily being clairvoyant, though that may be how it appears to less aware people. You are merely being insightful. Through intense observation, along with your other natural powers of analysis and instinct, you attempt to build up a picture of:

- why they do what they do.
- what they are feeling.
- what they want.
- how their words differ from their actions.
- what their actions tell you.
- what is not being said.
- what it is like to be that person, rather than yourself.

Successful leaders do not act in a vacuum. They are constantly scanning for signals to suggest what to do next. Be a kind of detective, using your curiosity and interest to make sense of what is needed. Successful leaders can often mentally put themselves in their followers' shoes and guess how they will respond to different situations.

You can even do this physically. Understanding body language, for instance, concerns your ability to stand back and watch. That though, is only the first step. To really understand another person, it helps to try and emulate their posture, gestures or expression. Privately imitate the person and see what it feels like to walk around and express yourself in the way that they do. You may acquire some really valuable clues about how they tick.

Best of all, ask them! It's surprising how often this simple way of gaining a better understanding of others is neglected in favour of more elaborate and time-consuming methods. People will often tell you what they intend. By not asking them, you ignore an essential source of information.

Channels

You cannot expect to always understand people by communicating through formal channels or even solely at work. You may occasionally need to sacrifice valuable personal time to socialise in non-work settings.

Famous leaders have often abandoned their own security in favour of hearing directly from their followers' own lips.

The founder of Walmart in America regularly arrived at selected stores around 6 a.m. or 7 a.m. That way he could meet employees starting their day and spend time talking to them before they got too involved with their work.

Even when you think you have gained a clear picture of what other people are thinking, feeling or saying, you may need to check it for accuracy. This means testing your conclusions by asking them whether your view of what they think and feel is correct. Start conversations with some provocative question, for example, 'I was wondering how you felt about the current changes?' or 'You seem to be a bit quiet today, is there anything going on?'

As long as such questions are asked in an unthreatening way, you may well unearth some crucial information that will help avoid unmotivated behaviour and wasted effort.

Understanding others is a continuous process of:

- observation,
- exploration, and
- testing.

PERCEPTIONS OF SITUATIONS

We view the world through our own mental maze, established over many years. No two people ever see the world identically because of their different experiences, expectations or wishes. This makes a leader's job particularly hard, since communicating to people about a situation, for instance, may challenge their unique perceptions about it.

Effective leaders see:

- reality, and
- new possibilities.

Leaders see things differently from other people. Their reality is not always more objective or accurate, but usually more strongly held. Powerful leaders enable others to see the world through their eyes.

When an effective leader says 'this is the situation', we may not necessarily agree, yet we can respond to this interpretation, because it makes sense to us.

So, for example, a majority of us might think that newspapers are about disseminating information and news. However, business leader Rupert Murdoch has seen a different reality—that newspapers are more about entertainment. Those who work for him come to see the same reality.

How do leaders arrive at a different reality? It comes from using a different set of criteria for judging the world. This might include adopting new or discarding old:

- views,

- prejudices,

- assumptions,

- beliefs, and

- interpretations.

Through their clear perception of the present situation, leaders 'see' what is needed. They do so by being alert, paying more attention, and so are able to 're-frame' the situation until it makes sense to them and ultimately to others.

Leadership also means seeing things as they might be in the future. If managing is organising what already exists, then leadership is about creating possibilities and moving towards something that does not exist.

How can you improve your capacity to see new possibilities? Do it by expanding your creative activity in the widest sense. If you value creativity, you are more likely to have a significant impact on others. Leaders apply their natural creative powers to see new possibilities.

To develop your foresight is to comprehend:

- how can we stay ahead of the game.

- what new developments are on the horizon.

- what unexpected situations might we plan for.

- what if the current trends were reversed.

Looking for alternatives, seeking examples that seemingly contradict current organisational culture, noting where the rules are being broken productively, may all help your ability to see what is not yet manifest. Ask your colleagues:

- What are you working on that's new or different?

- If we had a magic wand, how could we transform things around here?

- How could we make things ten times better around here?

Just as it is useful to put yourself in others' shoes and see things from their point of view, so it helps if you can stand outside a situation. Seeing it from afar often allows you to grasp the bigger picture, preventing you from becoming enmeshed in detail. This wider perspective allows you to see where things are going, or how they are developing, rather than being stuck in the current situation.

Practice

Everything to do with leadership insight takes practice. Certainly, some people may have been born more intuitive than others. Yet by practising observation, trying to understand other people, attempting to see reality and imagining the future, you can develop insight.

Spend some time each day just looking. Do value this time as an essential part of the business. In these periods of reflection, you may well gain an insight that could save or earn your organisation huge profits—far more than the day-to-day slog of repetitive activities. That's what leaders contribute.

The seven 'I's of leadership need these paradigms.

- Taking responsibility

- Taking risk

- Direct action

- Vitality

While there are many different types of leadership styles, most people agree on these basic types.

- Autocratic or authoritarian

- Benevolent autocrat

- Consultative democratic

- Participatory democratic

- Delegate or free reign

```
                    Leadership Styles

  Authoritarian      Participative       Laissez-faire
   leadership         leadership          leadership

High level        <------------------------>    Low level
of control                                       of control
```

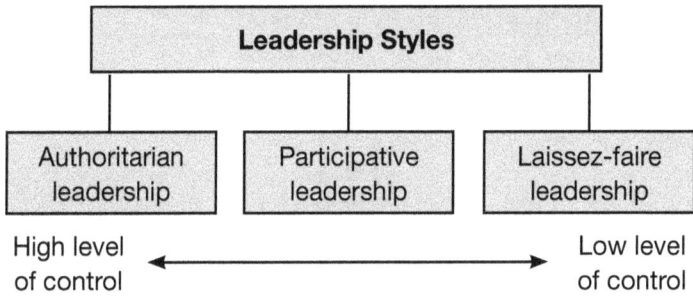

Each of these styles has their place or use. A good leader knows when to use a particular approach in a given situation.

4

Initiatives

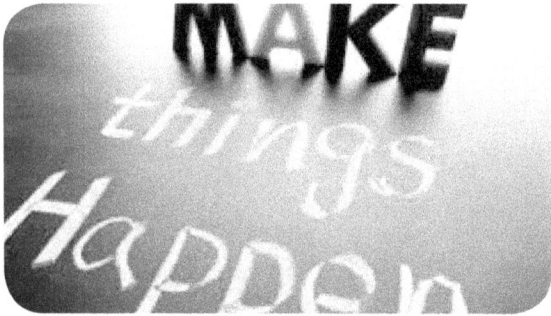

Leaders are people who make things happen, who take initiative and persuade others to join their cause. Initiatives support work and develop interest in contemporary organisations and leaders. Initiative will strengthen the infrastructure for leadership. This entails focus on leadership, competitive strategy, workforce management, organisational change and learning, ethics, diversity, global management, entrepreneurship, governance, negotiation, and the relationship between business and society.

You can exercise these skills anywhere, inside a company, in a voluntary organisation or a public agency, within a team or on the shop floor.

Initiative really means the act of setting a process in motion; ability or willingness to take the lead; right or duty to make the first move; enterprise; and capacity for acting independently or showing originality.

Use initiative by:

- responsibility,

- risk,

- direct action, and

- vitality.

RESPONSIBILITY

When a project fails, a leader takes responsibility. He says, 'I was beaten' he does not say 'My men were beaten'.

You can usually spot someone showing leadership by when they seem ready to take responsibility. People with leadership potential put themselves forward, or they offer to help others, who seek their guidance.

Look for opportunities to take responsibility through:

- volunteering,

- participating,

- being accountable, and

- taking centre-stage.

Volunteering

Volunteering is when you keep saying 'yes' whenever a job needs doing, or a problem needs another to solve it. Leaders willingly take things on, often the worst jobs or the ones with least apparent kudos. The act of taking initiatives forward, demonstrates leadership.

The ability to hone existing skills or develop new skills through a skill-based volunteer experience is in alignment with the basic premise of adult learning theory that suggests that these conditions are needed for optimal learning.

- Involvement in the planning and evaluation of instruction

- Relevance of content to their job or professional life

- Experiential activities

- Problem-centred rather than content-centred emphasis

Development through skill-based volunteering is about stretching one's skills and talents to meet the demands of a particular organisational project or goal. The more leadership or ownership the employee has on a particular project, the greater the potential for learning.

For example, when you say 'Yes, I'll do that' you set an example for others. You are indicating that 'this is how it should be around here'. By volunteering you demonstrate how you believe others should perform and inspire them to take responsibility too.

Volunteering also provides opportunities to learn and grow. You open yourself to new experiences and to change. Sometimes you do not know what you are letting yourself in for. Non-leaders play it safe and avoid volunteering.

There is always the danger of overdoing it, taking on excessive work. This is destructive. Only you can judge whether you can handle more or are heading for burn out. Avoiding opportunities and playing safe, though, stops personal challenges that help you realise your own potential.

Participating

Another test of your leadership potential is whether you take part in other people's projects. Your willingness to join a task force, a project group, a committee, a team activity, is an important sign of leadership in an organisation.

It is active not passive participation that builds leadership. Merely going along with the crowd is compliance. Active participation is demonstrating by your actions and behaviour that 'I want to contribute.'

Being accountable shows that you can be relied upon. First you make statements, such as:

- 'I'll' see that gets done.'
- 'Leave that to me.'
- 'That was my fault.'
- 'I'll solve that.'
- 'I got that wrong.'
- 'I'll complete that on time.'
- 'Nobody else is handling this, so I will.'
- 'I take responsibility for that.'

Now you have to back up these promises with actions that support them.

When you act as a leader, people tend to say 'She does what she says she'll do' or 'You can rely on him to do that.' By showing that you are willing to stand up and be counted, you put your personal values on public display.

When a serious mistake occurs, do not try to pass the buck on to someone else. Instead, be willing to shoulder some or all of the blame. People will tend to see you as willing to accept criticism as well as praise. Accountability could even be taking the blame for something that is not your fault. For example, if someone responsible to you makes a serious error, as a leader, you cannot hide behind them and say 'I didn't do it.' To some degree you too are in the firing line.

Unlike managers, leaders never justify what they do solely by referring to rules, company policy, job descriptions, written briefs and other ways of denying responsibility.

Taking Centre Stage

Taking centre stage is another aspect of taking responsibility. You allow your leadership to be seen and acknowledged. Although some leaders can be self-effacing, ultimately all are willing to stand in the limelight.

Leaders we admire tend not to place themselves at the centre of things, instead they place others there. They do not seek attention so much as give it to others. However, they are prepared to be in the limelight when necessary. Occasionally the limelight is more intense, when events bring you into the public eye and attract the attention of the media. Leading means being prepared to be visible in whatever form matters take. You cannot both lead and shirk from taking responsibility.

5

Stepping Out
Of The Comfort Zone

It can be quite uncomfortable being a leader. In fact, what separates leaders from their supporters is:

- stepping out of the comfort zone,

- being non-compliant, and

- handling rejection, disagreement and failure.

Step Out Of The Comfort Zone

Stepping out of the comfort zone happens by attempting something unfamiliar, where you are unsure about the outcome.

Stepping out of the comfort zone is when you:

- disagree.

- say things that may upset people.

- do things that attract disapproval.

- break the rules.

- challenge convention.

- try new things.

- do what is right, rather than what is convenient.

- question received wisdom.

- act without always knowing all the likely outcomes.

- deliberately put yourself in a learning situation.

- seek information on how others see you.

- commit to action without knowing if others will follow.

Your comfort zone is the area of experience where you know what to expect and how you are likely to perform. While it may be a congenial place, it is also a limiting one. It shuts you off from all sorts of experiences, feedback and situations that might help you grow and develop as a person and as a leader.

Leaving your comfort zone involves new situations where you do not know the rules or are unsure of how you will fare. Try giving yourself some systematic practice at this. For example, list twenty challenging things you would like to do, yet have never done before.

These risks might be:

- physical,
- social,
- emotional,
- political,
- breaking a habit, or
- presenting yourself in an unusual way, etc.

Challenging your own habits and patterns makes you more open to other people, to hearing what they say, to learning what they want. Besides, it stops you from merely going through life on auto-pilot.

Can you think of some activities that would develop you and make you feel stretched and challenged? They may be slightly daunting or might involve doing something you have often delayed.

It is time to get some fresh stimulus from talking to colleagues, going on a course, or whatever it will take to start the ball rolling.

Yet another way of exploring your present comfort zone is to begin deliberately breaking old patterns and habits. These are not necessarily wrong, but may merely stop you from seeing the world afresh, limiting your vision and no longer providing stimulus.

For example, do you always take the same route home every day? Try three different ways and notice what you learn or how it stimulates you. If you always read one type of newspaper, drink one brand of lager, get up the same time often, experiment with doing it differently for a month. If you always tend to work late, try having a whole week in which you go home early.

List some of your more obvious patterns or habits. You may need someone close to you to help you spot some of these. Having identified half a dozen, find ways to break them and see how you feel. If even thinking about doing so makes you uncomfortable, it could be a good reason for taking action.

Non-compliance

Being non-compliant is the need to assert yourself. By being unassertive, you are failing to say what you think and feel, or not attempting to do what you want. By contrast, leaders continuously express what they want and communicate it, until they are heard.

While sometimes it's sensible to conform, there may be occasions when you should really listen to your own impulses to express yourself strongly. Do you tend to sit on these impulses and say nothing?

Speaking the truth

Leadership is speaking your truth, even when others may strongly disagree. It is being able to say 'no' to the crowd, doing what you think is right, even if it means being different.

Generally, managers do things right or 'correctly' by following the rules. Leaders, though, take the risk of deciding for themselves what is right and do it, often regardless of any rules or the expectations of others.

Handling rejection

Few people succeed in life without some setbacks or finding that some people disagree with them. Leaders are ready to risk the experience of people failing to support them.

Unless you ask people to do something, you may never know whether they will follow your wishes. Should they refuse or fail to commit themselves wholeheartedly, you may feel abandoned, betrayed or ignored. How do leaders cope with these negative experiences?

Effective leaders never allow setbacks to dent their self-confidence or to stop them heading in the direction they want to go. Faced with setbacks, they are noticeably resilient. It is often in adversity that true leadership emerges. We all know the ironical fact: Any fool can steer the ship when the sea is calm.

Try exploring how you handle rejection and disagreement. When was the last time things didn't go your way? Do you allow your reactions to undermine your leadership confidence?

Fostering self-confidence

Fostering your own and others' self-confidence is not just about being positive. When you communicate your belief that you will succeed or that your supporters can be successful, you help them to extend themselves and to persevere.

The best leaders keep their morale up in the face of rejection or failure by:

- persistence,

- not personalising, and

- reframing.

Persistence

Effective leaders never seem to give up, continue their particular vision, long after others have fallen by the wayside. Persistence has its own reinforcing effect on emotions. Sheer determination can drown out the siren voices of negativity. When you are persistent despite obstacles and setbacks, you start to become inspirational.

Excessive persistence, though, can become obduracy and be unhelpful. If you keep ignoring the reality around you, blindly continuing against all the evidence, you risk rejection.

Not personalising setbacks

Not personalising your setbacks is another key to dealing with rejection. Because you will face many setbacks in your leadership, it is important not to treat them as aimed at you personally. Often they are merely the result of forces beyond your immediate control. Try talking to an uninvolved person to gain a fresh perspective when your leadership seems to be meeting problems. Even leaders need mentors sometimes.

Reframing

Reframing is yet another way of dealing with setbacks and disagreements. Here, you take a situation and restate it in new ways. For example, suppose you suggest that your company's computer system needs updating because it is out-dated and slow. If this proposal is rejected, rather than abandon it, you might start to reframe the issue as a need for better communications and ways of keeping in touch with customers. From this might eventually flow a greater readiness to consider a new system.

6

Direct Action

> Leadership is not a position or a title; it is an action and example.

The options are clear: "'Lead", "follow" or "get out of the way".'

Sometimes ideas become bogged down by bureaucracy, apathy or natural resistance. No amount of talking achieves a breakthrough and something else is needed. Effective leaders recognise these situations and have a bias for action, a tendency to say 'enough talking, here's what we're going to do'.

Use your instinct and observation to decide when to stop talking and start acting.

To get things moving, leaders willingly risk criticism, reprimands or worse. Direct action means making something happen, sometimes regardless of whether this has immediate benefits. Often the decision provides the essential leverage to move forward. Leaders realise that there are occasions when a decision—any decision—is better than none at all.

Leadership is not good or bad, it is how you use it!

Community and labour organising models place a high value on leadership and leadership development. They know that leaders are critical for moving people to action.

Leadership is influencing people—by providing purpose, direction and motivation—while operating to accomplish the mission and improving the organisation.

Influence is a means of getting people to do what you want them to do. It is the means or method to achieve two ends: operating and improving. But there's more to influencing than simply passing orders. The example you set is just as important as the words you speak. And you set an example—good or bad—with every action you take and every word you utter, on or off duty. Through your words and example, you must communicate purpose, direction and motivation.

SEVEN PRINCIPLES OF EFFECTIVE LEADERSHIP

Set An Example

Where leaders demonstrate honesty, hard work, courage and respect for others and show that they are willing to make personal sacrifices for the cause, those same characteristics will be evident among followers. Systematic corruption cannot be avoided when leaders are corrupt.

Know The People You Expect To Lead

An effective leader must demonstrate care and concern for those he/she is expected to lead. Leaders must create a climate of trust and show a willingness to listen. Community-level leaders should make an effort to personally know their supporters, as well as 'fence sitters', and make genuine effort to demonstrate concern for them.

Be Proficient In Carrying Out Responsibilities

Leaders are expected to articulate clearly why the struggle must be undertaken to inspire. They ought to be the resistance symbol instead of visible leadership.

Seek And Accept Responsibilities

Conflict environments are characterised by uncertainty, wrong judgements and mistakes. Effective leaders step forward with confidence and fill leadership voids that will appear when a movement experiences a setback. They also accept responsibility for failure if the movement does not achieve its objectives.

Give Others Credit For Success

Good leaders usually do not use the word 'I' when discussing a successful event. It was 'we' who succeeded. Thus, good leaders show people that they are in the very heart of the things and that their individual participation is what really makes a difference to the success of the struggle. They acknowledge and show appreciation for the participation and contributions of others.

Learn From Experiences

The most expensive way to learn is from your own mistakes. Thus, effective leaders learn from their own and others' lessons and successes.

Delegate Authority And Responsibility

A good leader never assumes that he/she is the only intelligent person in the movement. Successful leaders know how to challenge and maximise the abilities of subordinates. The right people should be selected for the right positions, and responsibilities for more strategic activities should extend down through the movement leadership, together with a process for delegating responsibility to subordinates. Even the best leaders in history had a twenty-four-hour-per-day limitation and their movements would have collapsed if they had tried to do all of the activities themselves. Over centralisation of decision-making is a fatal flaw in any organisation!

Leadership Development

Qualities to look for in a leader

- Team work—TEAM: Together Each Aim (is) Met

- Accessibility—don't just open the door; walk out of the door

- Accountability—leaders must be prepared to accept the accountability

- Respect people's time—lead with respect for time boundaries

- Pays attention to undercurrents—to positive dynamics, undercurrents

- Address issues directly—address well-known issues openly and directly

- Take initiatives but not all the space—be kinetic; space cannot be static

- Starts things but delegates—delegation is an essential leadership skill

- Can remain unattached to one's own vision—a visionary leader can motivate

- Collaborates

- Communicates with confidence about decisions— one who clearly and passionately communicates his or her vision can be an agent of change

- Can step back and let others lead—great leaders make space for others to shine

- Has integrity—this builds valuable trust between people

- Think critically—sharpen your own skills of effective critical thinking and utilise those

- Willing to work and get involved—set the bar, inspire and motivate

- Set goals—align yourself with constantly changing goals and priorities

- Believes in change and social justice—assumptions and core values of social justice, helps members of the organisation

- Ability to push co-workers—push employees to do their best

- Hard worker—don't undervalue hard work in leadership

- Unselfish—the cornerstone of leadership is the quality of unselfishness

- Not afraid—leaders are not afraid to fail

- Persuasive—essential skills of persuasion is a must

- Lead meetings in workplace—effective meetings are are reflective of overall of team functioning

- Trainer—corporate training programmes will teach you how to successfully take charge of your team in today's business world

- Responsible/Dependable—responsible leadership is a must for performance

- Be able to solve problems—leaders facilitate the team to solve problems

- Thinks of co-workers; cares for them—it's not about you; it is about them

- Honest—honesty is essential to a leader's legitimacy, credibility, and ability to develop

- Trustworthy—one must be trusted to lead

- Mutual respect with supervisors—supervisors create an atmosphere of mutual respect

- Persistent—be a persistent leader not a stubborn one

- Positive person; not a quitter—successful people never quit

- Listens—leaders must not just hear; they must listen

- Understands how the company works—one must understand work values and culture of the company

- Can communicate with others—relay messages

- Can and willing to learn—good leaders never stop learning

- Can give and accept criticism—criticism is a natural part of leadership

Role Of A Leader

A good leader should:

- be a good listener.

- move people to action.

- communicate issues in the workplace.

- bring vision to co-workers.

- have knowledge of labour movement.

- be educated on issues, union, and what co-workers do.

- be eyes and ears of the unions.

- help interpret to co-workers what the boss is doing.

- delegate responsibilities.

- recruit more leaders and get people involved.

- lead by example.

- confront the boss.

- represent union in public; be a spokesperson.

- give/contribute ideas.

- attend actions and meetings.

- be a bridge to co-workers.

- know the workplace.

- assess co-workers.

Developing Leaders

- Motivate

- Commit

- Make a plan

- Support implementation

- Follow up and evaluate

Developing As Leaders

- Listen to potential leaders and ask questions.

- Talk directly about commitment and being a leader.

- Give assignments with details.

- Get workers to make a commitment to assignments.

- Congratulate team members/workers for completing an assignment.

VITALITY

Enthusiasm, high energy, vitality—exemplary leaders who deliver exemplary results have these characteristics.

Meet any effective leader and you are almost always struck by their vitality. It is a result of using their energy to stay wide awake, constantly alert and naturally curious.

Vitality is hard to define precisely though, like leadership itself, you certainly know it when you see it.

Enthusiasm rubs off on people!

Your vitality level may be low—especially if you are focusing on things like day-to-day surviving or the busyness of just getting by. Are you surviving or thriving?

Your vitality level may be more mid-level if you have the survival stuff handled and you are now working on things like enjoying a sense of belonging, becoming more social and nurturing a desire to do connect better. Low-and-mid-line vitality levels have a lot to do with getting our needs met—basic ones or otherwise. They are also indicative of times of transition.

If you already have your core needs met, then you are in a place of wanting to do more actualising and thriving and you are ready to grow and challenge yourself.

Seven ways to increase your personal leadership vitality

- Tap into what brings meaning.

- Tap into what brings satisfaction and joy.

- Tap into what brings ease.

- Tap into what brings effective performance.

- Tap into what brings 'aliveness'.

- Tap into what brings awareness of the present moment.

- Tap into what brings simplicity.

You cannot expect to have vitality unless you are healthy, which means paying attention to the needs of your body, mind and spirit. A healthy mind, indeed.

Busy people often neglect exercise without realising its contribution to their leadership potential. Regular exercise does more than just keep you fit. It's like air-conditioning for the brain. It blows away the mental cobwebs and contributes to your state of alertness.

Managers often pay lip service to maintaining a balance between work and non-work. Effective leaders, though, know a balance is essential for retaining their natural vitality.

Leisure and holidays are essential for sustaining leadership energy. It is all too easy to burn out from work. The very word recreation is about re-creating your vitality. The best leaders realise that they need to take care of themselves to minimise the impact of stress.

Work often makes an impact on who we are. Leaders create the work they want, rather than react to what is thrown at them. Being aware of the bigger picture of one's life is another powerful way of staying sane.

Vitality also stems from being open to personal growth and learning. To realise your full potential as a leader means discovering as much about yourself as possible, both your strengths and your own development needs.

Gaining the support of others is another important source of vitality. People love to be asked for their help. You can only create supporters by making room for people's contribution.

Being willing to say 'I don't know' is also a sign of strength, rather than weakness, as long as it's not a constant theme in your conversations. Allow yourself to be nurtured by others around you. To lead, you do not need to be omnipotent.

7

Inspiration

> Great leaders inspire greatness in others!

Leaders inspire, managers motivate. It is perfectly possible to survive as a manager without ever inspiring anyone. However, you cannot be a leader without the ability to inspire.

What is inspiration? In essence, it's a feeling, an experience. We are moved in some way. Its result is that people feel different and are willing to do unusual things.

They go beyond their present limits, show courage, deal with formidable odds, and cope with impossible circumstances.

Often the most basic experiences can be unbelievably inspiring, such as a daily sunset or the birth of a child. In business, inspiration usually enables people to perform beyond their normal limits, to go that extra mile, produce outstanding results and look forward to coming to work. Inspiration mostly comes from the excitement of living. It comes from anything that quickens you to the instant.

Traditionally, we associate inspiration as the preserve of artists or charismatic personalities. Yet when anyone has a good idea or feels strongly about something, they can be inspiring for other people. When someone is inspired, it is as if they have received a spark of genius from some other world. Such moments may appear to be totally fortuitous, but often they come as a result of a period of intense work.

You can learn to inspire other people, not once but often. The inescapable starting point is: *To inspire others, first inspire yourself.*

Discovering what inspires you is always the first step to having an impact on other people. Making this discovery means you need to:

- immerse yourself in what seems to get you excited, moves you, makes you feel uplifted.
- be willing to explore what inspires others.
- start making a list of events, poems, works of art, films, books, people, plays, scenery or whatever that inspire you.
- start distinguishing between the mediocre and the inspirational.

Leaders work hard at inspiration and know that it doesn't always come easy. Make a choice to spend as much time as you can with whatever helps you, above the mundane.

When you are inspired, you are passionate, persuasive, un-self-conscious and a great communicator. Everyone has that potential; leaders just do it more often. Although one cannot reduce it to a simple formula, the common elements are:

- vision,

- communication,

- passion, and

- trust.

VISION

All leaders create a compelling vision, one that promises to take their supporters to a new place. Then they show how to turn that vision into a reality. You do not need to be unusually prescient—it is more to do with defining what you want the future to look like.

Sometimes we resist working with vision because we think it is the privilege of only gifted people.

Where does vision come from? It would be wonderful to wake up one morning with a compelling one and doubtless some exceptional leaders do work that way. However, more often, it requires a struggle to articulate vision and you may need help from your supporters to:

- identify the vision.

- expand the vision.

- translate the vision into a message that everyone can understand.

Vision operates in companies on three distinct levels:

- strategic,

- tactical, and

- personal.

Strategic Vision

Strategic vision is the organisation's overriding philosophy and provides the framework into which all activities fit. Somebody has to hold this vision, never losing sight of it. A strategic vision in business is not enough. As a leader, you will need to be concerned with both the tactical and personal aspects.

Tactical Vision

Tactical vision is the philosophy in action and provides people with clear methods for taking action. Often tactical vision helps one understand how the strategic vision will be achieved. Try to value quality above all else.

Personal Vision

Personal vision exists when each person in their own unique way starts acting so as to realise the vision.

A prevalent myth is that vision is always the invention of a single leader. It is more frequently the result of groups of people working in harmony towards a common aim. Arriving at the common aim may be difficult as people strive to create a joint picture of the future that inspires them. The leadership role is simply to wheel this creative process.

Another way of tapping into your own or your team's vision is to explore your own values. These are your core beliefs that you do not easily alter. You can begin to determine them by answering the question: What matters to you? Is it waste, injustice, poverty, happiness, love, winning or what? Try making a list of the five most important values in your life. Use these to help you begin building a picture of your vision of the future you want to create.

Many managers who are potential leaders fail through their impatience with the whole concept of vision. Because it is conceptual, they don't take the time to develop and refine it. Those who are more action-minded tend to reject it as 'airy-fairy stuff' or insufficiently connected with the real world.

Yet there is nothing more real than a compelling vision. People 'see' what could be and are prepared to do extraordinary things to realise it. Such people do not just 'look'; they 'see'.

8

Communication

LEADERSHIP COMMUNICATION

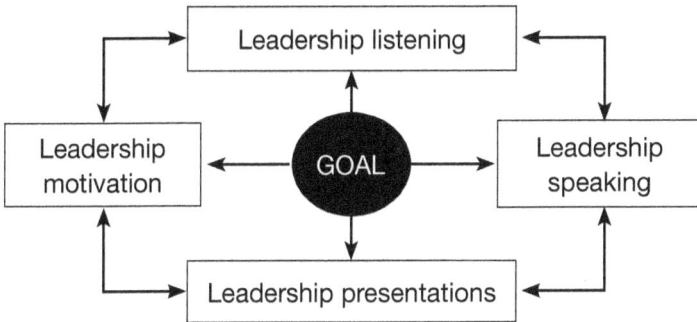

A vision that stays within your head is useless. If you really care about your vision, you will want to share it with others. It will inspire and excite you to the point where you cannot help telling other people about it.

Most effective managers are good communicators and leaders are even better at it. You do not need to persuade a leader that presentation matters or that their message needs to have an impact. They are already convinced. You may well need to refine your communication skills if you are to lead successfully. You can do this in several ways.

- Think visually
- Use specific and practical examples
- Keep your messages short
- Explain the likely results of what you want
- Show personal commitment
- Ceaselessly talk about your vision to others
- Listen carefully
- Practise new ways of explaining your leadership message

Thinking visually means developing ways of conveying your vision to build pictures in people's minds. Strive to create an image of what you want, an almost tangible visualisation of how the future should look. This requires practice. Start by thinking of images that already strike you as powerful, whether these are advertising pictures, paintings, a scene from a film or a photograph from a book.

What image would summarise the future you want to create? Finding a powerful image or an interesting metaphor to describe it, helps other people 'see' what you are seeking.

Use specific and practical examples to bring your vision to life. People understand messages best through real instances to which they can personally relate. For instance, by telling people how they will be affected by what you want to do, you are starting to turn vision into a reality.

Keep your messages short to avoid clogging the communication channels. This is not the same as being a person of few words. Effective leaders realise that at any one moment people can only absorb a certain amount of information. They become experts at reducing their communication to extremely simple ideas.

Explain the likely results of what you want. People need to understand how they will be affected by what you want to achieve. Use examples to bring these results to life. Suppose a company's vision is that it should be the customer's first choice, this might start to be translated into practical tasks such as always ensuring that the phone is answered within three rings.

Show personal commitment to what you want to achieve. This can be summed up as sharing your feelings with supporters; ceaselessly talk about your vision to others. Leaders persistently talk about what they want, what matters, and what the vision is all about. Getting your message across requires constant communication. Just keep watching for any opportunity to share your ideals.

Listen carefully to what others have to say about your vision. This will help you refine it. Communication is a two-way process and merely bragging on about your idea stops you from receiving some invaluable input. Let people play devil's advocate with your idea. It will help you clarify it and make you even more able to communicate it effectively.

Effective communication skills do not come naturally to most people. Many people, including business leaders and managers, need to practise in order to improve their skills.

There are three over-arching skills that lead to success.

- Self-communication skills

Self-communication is the internal dialogue we have all day long and it is directly reflected by our attitude. Procrastination is often a direct result of negative self-communication.

- Private, one-on-one communication skills

  The key to face-to-face communication is building trust.

- Public/Group communication skills

  Skilled public speakers use powerful body language, add value to the audience and are great storytellers.

PASSION

Passion in leadership is about first becoming absolutely convinced of the importance of what you want and then being totally willing to share that strong feeling with others.

Passion is what powerful leaders have in large measure. They also insist on sharing it, constantly. Their passion is not directionless. It is sharply focused around what they want to achieve. It is concentrated and, like a laser beam, cuts through objections, obstacles and negativity. It is hard to say 'No' to someone who cares so strongly about something and difficult to resist being drawn into their vision and becoming engaged.

In business, it is now more acceptable to talk of commitment or conviction than it was a decade ago. Effective leaders soon learn that it is passion that moves people to support them, not appeals to logic or a recital of facts and figures.

Passion truly works when you are emotionally connected to what you want. When you make that connection, you sound convincing and others find their emotions engaged too.

Start by listing your passions. When you substitute your emotions, you are also vulnerable since you are sharing with others what really matters to you. If they reject what you want, in some sense they seem to be rejecting you too.

Passionate leaders are not afraid of letting their feelings come through. You can only expect to move others if you are willing to be moved yourself. This does not necessarily mean you are reduced to a tearful mess, though more than one leader has allowed tears to flow in the heat of the moment.

TRUST

Leaders who inspire trust, garner better output, morale, retention, innovation, loyalty and revenue.

To inspire people to participate, they need to trust both you and themselves. For this:
- trust yourself,
- do what you say you will do, and
- trust others.

When you trust yourself, you are willing to:
- listen to that inner voice.
- use your instincts.
- allow feelings to play an important, though not necessarily always dominant, part in guiding your actions.

The bottom line is loud and clear: The only way to make a man trustworthy is to trust him.

The perfect leader builds trust slowly, starting small. For example, you create trust in others when you always do what you say you will do—because effective leaders honour their word. They are consistent in their approach and policy. Thus leaders partly attract people because they can be relied upon. When you are reliable, people will naturally tend to ask for your opinion, seek your help, and follow your guidance.

Having developed trust in yourself and shown that you trust others, you are ready to move on to helping people learn to trust each other. If you lead a team, for example, this is a crucial part of your job. There may be many creative ways you can discover to engender this trust, some of which may work more quickly than others.

Where mutual trust does not exist, people are cautious, less open, less influential, more distant and more inclined to leave at the first opportunity. True leadership is getting ordinary people to do extraordinary things. That's inspirational.

INVOLVEMENT

Managers devolve, leaders involve. It takes real leadership for people to feel genuinely part of a vision and fully committed to realising it. Too often, only lip service is paid to the idea of involving people.

There are various ways to begin involving people in what you want to achieve.

- Enrolment

- Empowerment

- Personal investment

- Feedback

Enrolment

Trying to force someone's enrolment is like shouting 'grow' at a plant. While it may sound impressive, it is unlikely to achieve much. Effective enrolment occurs when someone 'buys into' what you want to achieve. That is, they take the important step of saying 'Yes, I'd like to be part of that'. In effect, they are 'signing on'.

Empowerment

'When the best leader's work is done, the people say: "We did it ourselves",' said Lu-Tzu.

Leadership by just issuing orders and attempting to control everything has never really worked well in business organisations for long. Leadership is about sharing power, giving support to others so they feel inspired to do great things.

In fact, empowerment means giving people responsibility, the right to make decisions and take charge of their lives.

When people have the autonomy to take over all aspects of management, including work, holiday scheduling, ordering materials and hiring new team members, the results are nearly always spectacular gains in productivity and creativity.

Paradoxically, by releasing some of your leadership authority, you actually enhance it. People then feel more able to ask for your help, to hear your suggestions and to follow your lead. Some of the known results include:

- revitalised employees,
- boost in morale,
- increased productivity, and
- improved quality.

There are innumerable ways to empower through your leadership. Just be creative in discovering which ones work best for you and your supporters. Successful approaches include:

- showing people that they are not separate from the management and that they can help the organisation improve.
- demonstrating that good ideas are implemented.
- appreciating and rewarding suggestions even if they are not implemented.
- trusting people with responsibility.
- respecting people's ideas and judgement.
- allowing people to make decisions.

Personal Investment

Enrolment and empowerment are easier to achieve when people have a personal investment in the vision or purpose. This is not necessarily financial investment. It is a process of putting some important aspects of themselves into the work, such as:

- time,
- energy,
- creativity,
- ideas,
- know-how,
- personal resources including information and contacts,
- personal development,
- formal training, and
- creating important relationships.

Check on the personal investment your supporters are making. People who have made a personal investment are less likely to fail when the going gets tough.

When you demonstrate that you too have a major personal investment in the vision or purpose, others are more likely to follow. When you enlist people's personal investment, you do not need to motivate them, they are already motivated.

Feedback

Leaders need continual feedback on how they are doing and the best ones keep seeking out this information from innumerable channels, both formal and informal.

Feedback is how people influence a leader's plans and contribute to the vision. If you try doing this without this essential information, you risk being on the receiving end of some nasty, and for your leadership perhaps fatal, surprises.

Ensure that your own performance is continually monitored.

Hearing others' opinions is an invaluable resource and the best leaders are hungry to hear what people have to say about them.

The difference between
'You should have…' and
'Next time please…' is
called leading.

Leadership
Feedback

9

Improvisation

Improv!

A 'try it' environment!

There are no cast-iron rules of leading. Even if there were, they would certainly alter once you began relying on them. Instead, expand your ability to improvise, to think on your feet, to be creative in any moment, and respond to what is around you. That way you too can do it like it has never been done before. This is how you lead people in a rapidly changing world.

Doing it like it has never been done before is one of the most important aspects of business leadership.

When leaders improvise, they use:

- creativity,
- flexibility, and
- presence.

CREATIVITY

Creativity is to think of alternate options in a given situation. We usually think of creativity in simple terms, such as being an artist, or perhaps generating lists of new ideas. In fact, leadership creativity is much wider and includes many different aspects of doing things differently. It requires you to:

- innovate,

- stimulate others,

- create a 'try it' environment,

- solve problems, and

- receive and reward others' ideas.

Innovation

Innovation often means making something from nothing. Leaders take limited resources and weld them into new combinations, so that something original or different can emerge. In business, this mainly happens through identifying key issues and creating powerful teams, project groups, alliances and networks.

The leadership impulse to innovate, stems from the drive to initiate.

- How do I best tap my natural creativity?

- What triggers my creativity?

- When do I get my ideas?

- How do I usually respond to other people's creativity?

- How often do I take out time for reflection?

Leadership creativity also stems from enabling others to be innovative and original. Study how to trigger creativity in individuals and teams. Everyone can do it; they may just need a stimulus. Leaders provide the stimulus.

Discovering what triggers a team's creativity, for example, gives you a powerful tool for making things happen. It is therefore worth learning what works and what does not.

Your leadership contribution is to provide relevant challenges that stimulate people to find new resources within themselves to create. Even if you genuinely believe they can do this, it is not enough by itself. Communicate it, showing clearly that you have faith in their innate ability to achieve breakthroughs.

At the heart of creativity lies the freedom to experiment and make mistakes. It is a hard freedom for some organisations to tolerate. The drive for fault-free, quality actions may conflict with the right to make mistakes and learn from them.

The following underpin the freedom to experiment.

- Clarifying the learning

- Not punishing people for mistakes

- Underlining that the only unacceptable mistakes are ones that could 'hole the ship below the waterline'.

When you focus on 'what can we learn from this mistake?' rather than 'who's to blame?' you ensure that lessons are not lost for the future. This helps to make your company a 'learning organisation'. Cherish mistakes as invaluable opportunities for learning.

Punishing people for mistakes is a great way to kill ideas. Once people realise they will suffer retribution when things go awry, they soon learn to play it safe. This is fine if you see an organisation merely as a machine, with the people in it merely cogs. However, this approach is almost certainly bound to fail in our fast moving world where it is often more important to be flexible than to always get things right.

The freedom to make mistakes is not a licence to be reckless. You do not ignore mistakes by simply shrugging your shoulders and saying 'that's too bad'. Rather, you use them as an opportunity to encourage yet more learning, to get it right next time, and to build fail-safe systems.

Try adopting the principle that people can make mistakes but are not permitted to 'hole the ship below the waterline'. This has stood the test of time. The more you personally commit to the idea of experimentation, the better. Involve your team, customers and other stakeholders in your experiments so that they all share the success and any possible failure.

Offer hypotheses for people in the organisation to test. For example, you might suggest that there is a growing market for a new type of service. Presenting this as a hypothesis for testing makes it more likely that you will uncover the truth, rather than having your supporters merely trying to prove you right.

Problem-solving

Most work is about solving problems in some form. The more interesting the problem, the more absorbing the work. Most problems are solved easily in the everyday activity of work, using information gained while solving previous problems. Occasionally though, problems arise that are tricky and these are the ones that leaders usually face. Such problems normally have few precedents, requiring a creative response.

Brainstorming, in which you produce lots of ideas without initially criticising or rejecting them, can start your natural, subconscious creative powers working. So, involve others and practise 'playing' with the problem. A sense of fun and a light-hearted approach can often release unforeseen solutions for even the most serious difficulties. Focus on solutions, not obstacles; receive and reward others' ideas.

Companies and teams are full of good ideas, though half of them never get beyond their office doors. As a leader, it's your responsibility to find ways of communicating that moves any new method from source to where it's needed. Suggestion boxes, email systems, open communication— every method can be used to process good ideas so that they can be used quickly.

FLEXIBILITY

People have a habit of persistently pursuing actions even when they are patently not getting anywhere. The first rule of holes is: if you're in one, stop digging.

Improvisation is about flexibility. Being able to adjust and adapt to situations is one of our prime abilities as human beings. Flexible thinking lets us resist primitive impulses to carry on regardless of the evidence.

Water is a great symbol of flexible power. If it cannot follow a direct course, it will always find a way through, winding around and adapting to the terrain. Yet its power will always move it onwards.

Clarity

The clearer your vision, purpose or objective, the easier it becomes to be flexible in how you achieve it. Not only may there be many routes to your destination, you may even invent ones that never before existed. By always focusing on the end result, you retain the larger picture. Leaders hold the picture as their guiding star.

Openness

Being open to people's ideas can supply you with more choices, some of which may be better than others. Releasing control generates other possibilities. Improvisation creates new solutions. Go with the flow of events, rather than always pushing against them.

When a leader shows flexibility, this helps avoid a frenzied reaction to any obstacle and promotes a creative response; responding means taking responsibility for using new information and putting it to work.

To respond productively so that you can improvise, you also need to be alert and present.

PRESENCE

Great leaders have the knack of giving you their full attention, at least for a while. They seem to be present, seeing what's happening in the moment.

- Many leaders talk about every minute being an opportunity to move the business on, to transform the situation, to create something out of nothing. This implies an intense awareness of moment to moment, a sense of staying conscious to how life changes continually.

- Leaders develop a heightened awareness of those moments of life and how quickly they disappear. This means being sensitive and also using your senses, particularly:

  Seeing. Look around at what's happening now; be alert. Are there opportunities staring you in the face right now?

  Listening. We are sometimes so busy planning what we're going to say, that we don't listen. True listening is active, not a passive way of waiting for your turn to speak.

Notice how often you are listening to the voice in your head, rather than fully absorbing what is being said to you. Leaders listen with respect and purpose. They are always asking 'what can I hear that will move us forward and how can I contribute to it?'

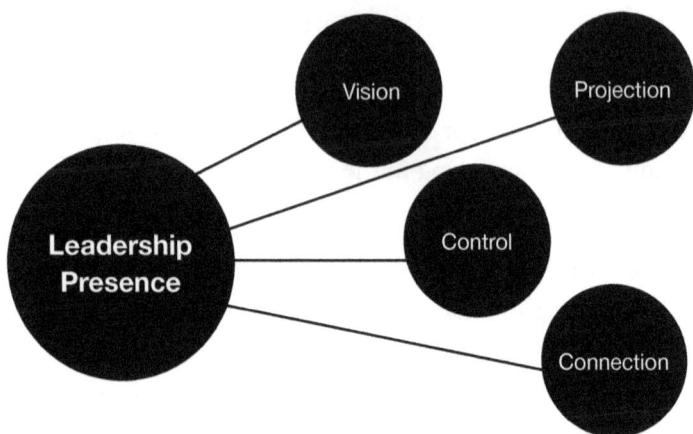

Impressive listening skills have been shown to be one of the common characteristics of credible leaders.

Work at becoming more aware of your feelings. These are clues to what excites you and others. Feelings help define the best decisions, what actions will inspire people, what's going on that others will want to be part of.

Individuality

Leaders are not afraid of being different, in most cases revelling in it!

Being different is a gift all of us possess, though not everyone cherishes it the way effective leaders do. Paradoxically, the best leaders convince people that they are one of them, yet also exceptional. Almost by definition, a leader stands out from others, if only by taking the lead. Leadership individuality stems from:

- being yourself,
- using personal experience,
- style,

- personal values,
- integrity, and
- building networks.

BEING YOURSELF

It is hard to be yourself, especially when pressure from the media, your friends and the organisation that you work for may make you feel that you are less important than what you do. Yet, who you are really matters! It is one of the crucial elements underpinning true leadership.

To be truly yourself is to possess considerable self-knowledge, which does not just 'happen'. It happens because you:

- are your own best teacher.
- accept responsibilities without blaming others.
- realise that you can learn anything you want to learn.
- reflect on your experiences.

It can be summed up as:

- being true to yourself, and
- accepting yourself with all your strengths and weaknesses.

When you accept who you are, you admire other people without trying to be them.

Two further aspects of being yourself are:

- a personal identity, and
- being distinctive.

The thing that makes you exceptional is inevitably that which must also make you lonely.

Personal Identity

Effective leaders possess a clear sense of their personal identity, linked to what they want—their destiny. Who they are defines what they want to achieve.

A clear sense of who you are lets you take risks and step out. Believing that whatever you do never fundamentally alters your essential 'self' means you are secure in your personal identity. You carve your own route and avoid over-compliance.

To be authentic is literally to be your own author, to discover your own native energies and desires and then to find your own way of acting on them.

There is no shortcut to achieving a strong personal identity. It's a journey of many years and you are already on it. However, you can choose to:
- stay aware of your journey.
- seek experiences that test and strengthen your identity.

PERSONAL EXPERIENCE

By winning a rat race, you will still remain a rat!

You are responsible for your own development and personal growth. No organisation can commit enough time or resources to you. The personnel or human resources department will only go so far in providing you with opportunities and training situations. It will never be quite enough.

You need some kind of personal plan to develop yourself and provide you with the kind of personal experience that will make you an effective leader. If you do not make one, probably no one else will. Even if they do, you are the only one really committed to making it work.

You already bring a wealth of personal history to the job of leading. Often this experience may have had little directly to do with actually leading. For example, your ability to understand and empathise with others comes from having shared similar experiences.

If people around you are facing chaos, success, uncertainty, triumph, despair—you are more able to lead them through these periods if you have encountered similar experiences. Our personal history provides us with some rich resources to deal with current problems.

Great leaders abandon old ideas and provide, first, a shock and then an inspiration for their followers. When Alexander cut the Gordian knot, rather than trying to unravel it, he was refusing to let past experience dictate how he solved the problem. His solution has inspired people ever since.

How can you capitalise on your personal experience? The simplest way is to always conduct a debriefing of every project—big or small. Dissect every failure, not to apportion blame but to comprehend what went wrong.

Personal style is another factor that distinguishes your way of leading from how others do it. Style is a combination of elements and actions which form a distinct pattern of consistent behaviour. Certainly, a leader's style is usually recognised by others.

Understanding how you come across to other people means exploring both the good and the bad elements of your style. There is your ability to listen, communicate clearly to get things done. Other aspects of your style may be less inspiring, such as your impatience, being late for meetings, your loss of the big picture when under pressure, and so on.

The strongest part of your style may be something that you least recognise or even value. Perhaps it is your humour or your caring that people find appealing about you as a potential leader. Only if you know and acknowledge these assets, can you capitalise on them.

Truly effective leaders want feedback from outside sources that see reality. Enlightened kings, for instance, hired advisers and travelling philosophers from foreign lands or visited them in their own territory.

PERSONAL VALUES

What comes to mind when someone says Marks and Spencer, Body Shop, IBM, SmithKline Beecham, the BBC and McDonald's? Each of these companies has strong values that influence how we regard them. Their values appear in everything they do and how they do it.

The same goes for leaders. What do you stand for? What do you really care about? What matters most to you? The answers will show up in your work, your possessions and in your relationships. Review all three and see if you can identify the values that matter. Are they of use to other people? Destructive values are unlikely to draw widespread support.

- Write out your personal credo or what matters to you
- Spend time clarifying your values
- Make values visible by behaving consistently

Being consistent with your values is where the phrase 'walk the talk' comes from. It means if you value quality, for instance, then it appears in everything you do; if you value people, you are seen as caring, someone who spends time with them. If you value efficiency, lead the way by being highly efficient yourself.

By talking about your personal values, you show you know your own mind. When you are faced with uncertainty or risk, your values enable you to proceed without direction or even approval from someone in authority. When as a leader you successfully share these values with others, you begin to help them make decisions and act independently.

INTEGRITY

Studies of managers confirm that the most frequent characteristic considered as essential for leadership is integrity. That is, leaders who are truthful, trustworthy, have character and convictions.

As a leader, personal integrity is doing what you say you will do.
- Uphold agreements
- Honour contracts
- Keep your word

Leaders with low personal integrity constantly break their word. They seldom last or are remembered, except with distaste.

Do people trust you? That is, do they believe that you'll do what you say you'll do and trust who you are?

This stems from people knowing that you are true to yourself, living your personal values as honestly as possible.

Gone are the days when leaders were meant to be superior beings, high-flown and haughty. These days, leaders need to be seen as real, down-to-earth and fully rounded human beings.

By knowing yourself sufficiently, you are able to accept who you are. It is this honest merging of all aspects of yourself that produces integrity. It is why you appear consistent to others.

'*The secret of success is consistency of purpose,*' said Benjamin Disraeli.

IMPLEMENTATION

What makes some leaders so unstoppable? Typically, it is their obsession for making things happen—sometimes at almost any price.

Talk about what you want to achieve—endlessly. Be willing also to devote limitless energy to ensuring your words are turned into deeds.

Successful leaders are implementation experts. They are fully aware that rhetoric is only a starting point. To be a leader, one:

- implements model behaviour.
- is action-minded.
- demands feedback.

- perseveres.
- celebrates success.

Achieving action is every leader's dream. Modern leadership requires high credibility because the old-style approach of using power and position to get what you want no longer really works. If you resort to these, you are not leading, you are dictating.

MODEL BEHAVIOUR

Example is leadership. You gain leadership credibility through practising what you preach. When you set an example, people believe what you say and start trying to emulate your example.

Showing through your own actions what you expect is a form of coaching. It conveys more convincingly than exhortations. It gives you an enormously powerful tool. You cannot lead from behind and expect people to be other than cynical about your leadership.

Nothing undermines a leader more than 'don't do as I do, do as I say'.

When you lead by example, you become highly visible. Great leaders do not need to be show-offs. They are willing to be seen and held accountable. There is no hiding as a leader, particularly in an age of rapid change and almost instant communication.

By leading through example, you:
- share your vision,
- promote your values, and
- show commitment to achieving results.

Leaders must be seen to be upfront, up to date and up to their job. They should:

- communicate clearly and succinctly.
- be open to suggestions.
- listen attentively.
- make sure everyone is involved.
- keep a grip on time.

11

Perseverance

> **SUCCESS IS NO ACCIDENT.**
> It is hard work, perseverance,
> learning, studying, sacrifice
> and most of all, **love** of what you are doing.
> - Pele

Sheer persistence often sets leaders apart from other people. They continue long after others have given up, abandoned hope or lost enthusiasm. This persistence eventually becomes a source of inspiration.

Credible leaders keep hope alive. They sustain it with their determination and higher aspirations. Fostering realistic yet optimistic attitudes, helps people to accept more challenging goals and achievements.

Perseverance comes from a deep belief in what you want to achieve. The clearer you are about this, the more likely that others will find your persistence attractive. By not easily giving up, leaders overcome obstacles that at first sight might seem unsurmountable.

The whole point of having support, involving others and creating networks is that it is hard to keep going sometimes. While the more passionate you are about your vision, the more likely you are to achieve it; there will always be moments of self-doubt or concern about the obstacles. During these times, you dig deep inside yourself to find that extra bit of commitment to persist.

Perseverance is a trait common among great leaders. One word describes quite possibly the most important of all leadership traits. That word is perseverance. It's only one word, but the depth and importance of that one word is limitless.

'I am convinced that about half of what separates the successful entrepreneurs from the non-successful ones is pure perseverance.'

Steve Jobs
1955-2011

12

Leadership: A Case Study

CASE 1

Humata (good thoughts), *hukhta* (good works) and *hvarshta* (good deeds) became the motto given by the Tata Group founder Jamsetji Nusserwanji Tata. In fact, it was designed on his coat of arms in 1869; it was the highest Zoroastrian principle. These values have been exemplified by the leadership of the Tata Group employees over the years. Their spirit exemplifies what Stephen Covey wrote: 'Management is efficiency in climbing the ladder of success; leadership determines whether the ladder is leaning against the right wall.'

This leadership was best demonstrated during the terror attack on the city of Mumbai. On 26 November 2008, terrorists attacked about a dozen locations in Mumbai, India, including one of the most iconic buildings in the city, the Taj Mahal Palace Hotel. For two nights and three days, the Taj was under siege, held by men with automatic weapons; they took some people hostage, killed others and set fire to the famous dome of the hotel. But amidst the gloom stood a silver lining: the leadership qualities even in a crisis of sorts. Apparently, something extraordinary had happened during the siege. According to hotel managers, none of the Taj employees had fled the scene to protect themselves during the attack. They all stayed at the hotel to help the guests. They made sure that each guest could find safety as they ferreted them out of the hotel, at grave risk to their own lives. The kitchen staff formed a human shield to assist guests who were being evacuated; they lost their lives as a result. The telephone operators after being evacuated chose to return to the hotel so that they could call guests and tell them what to do. Often during a crisis, a single hero or small group of heroes who take action and risk their lives will emerge. But what happened at the Taj was much broader. During the crisis, dozens of workers — waiters, busboys and room cleaners who knew back exits and paths through the hotel—chose to stay in a building under siege until their customers were safe. They were the very model of ethical, selfless behaviour. They exemplified leadership to the hilt. The example of the Taj and the incredible sacrifices of the employees who worked there is a very compelling, lesson of sorts.

Karambir Singh Kang, the General Manager of the Taj worked to save people even after his wife and two sons, who lived on the sixth floor of the hotel, died in the fire set by the terrorists. Kang's wife Nitti (thirty-eight years old) and two sons, Samar (fourteen years old) and Uday (five years old), who were put up at the sixth floor of the Heritage Wing of the iconic hotel were killed in the terror attack on 26 November that lasted for nearly sixty hours. Despite losing his family, Kang continued to supervise rescue operations and helped guests at the hotel. Forty-year-old Kang took charge as General Manager of Taj Mahal and Tower in November 2007 and had seventeen years of experience in the hospitality industry.

Kang lost his family in the most gruesome manner even as he himself was instrumental in rescuing many lives, including staff and patrons at the hotel. He was personally following rescue operations at the hotel, besides providing all help to security agencies even though he was not aware about the whereabouts of his family.

After the siege of Taj ended, Group Chairman Ratan Tata had asked Kang to take some rest but he preferred to stay at the scene and help in the operations. Not to be cowed down by the terrorists, Kang was at the side of Ratan Tata when he came to inspect the hotel on the day the encounter ended.

Kang, who had taken ashes of his wife and two children to Mohali, where he owns a farmhouse, mustered the courage to return to work but avoided talking to anybody as he was grief-stricken. Indeed, his demonstration of leadership—his coming back—was a befitting reply to terrorists.

> 'Take decisions and actions based on what you believe is the right thing to do—even if these actions are difficult or emotionally hard.' —*RATAN TATA*

CASE 2

The motto of the Central Reserve Police Force (CRPF) is 'Service and Loyalty'. This service came into existence as the Crown Representative's Police on 27 July 1939. After Independence, it became the Central Reserve Police Force on enactment of the CRPF Act on 28 December 1949. The CRPF is considered India's largest paramilitary force. It has a sanctioned strength of 3,08,862 personnel. Leadership is the ethos of each and every one on duty.

15 August 2016: 'It is a very important day.' These were the last words of CRPF Commandant Pramod Kumar after he unfurled the tricolour at the forces' base in Srinagar, minutes before he fell to militants' bullets in the Nowhatta area of the Jammu and Kashmir capital. Forty-four-year-old Kumar, Commanding Officer of the forty-ninth battalion of the CRPF deployed in the Kashmir valley, hoisted the flag between 8.30 a.m. and 8.40 a.m. and made a speech about India clocking seventy years of its freedom. He told his police personnel that the responsibility on security forces has 'increased' and that they have to effectively tackle militants and incidents of stone pelting in Jammu and Kashmir. Ironically, he was shot dead by terrorists an hour later. Just before he ended his speech, Kumar, in a video of the event, is seen looking at his watch as he said 'It is an important day', unaware of the fate that awaited him. The officer, who joined the paramilitary in 1998, also read out with pride the names of those personnel of the force who were awarded gallantry medals on the eve of the Independence Day and congratulated them. Soon after, officials said, the wireless set in the CRPF control room crackled informing about militants hurling grenades and firing on security forces

at four places in downtown Srinagar including Nowhatta Chowk, Gojwara Chowk, Bata Gali and Khanyar Chowk, as they sought reinforcements. Nothing could deter this icon of leadership. Kumar, along with a small team, dashed out in a bullet-proof vehicle and soon reached at the spot. The militants were still firing. Kumar led from the front and was shot grievously on the upper part of his neck but that was not before Kumar and his men eliminated the two militants. He was rushed to the 92 Base Hospital of the army in Srinagar, where he succumbed to his injuries. A senior CRPF officer, who had served with Kumar in the counter-insurgency grid in the Northeast earlier, described Kumar as very 'cool but daring'. We will never know why he said that it was an important day. Maybe he had some premonition of the events that unfolded in quick time. His leadership will remain inspirational for generations to come. Kumar was posted to Srinagar in April 2014 and was recently promoted as a Commandant. Kumar had been thrice decorated with the CRPF Director General's commendation in 2015, 2014 and 2011. He had earlier served in the Special Protection Group for three years. Most befittingly, gun salutes were paid to Late CRPF commandant Pramod Kumar during his last rites in Jamtara (Jharkhand) on 16 August 2016. Hundreds of people gathered outside his home to pay homage. But it was his seven-year-old daughter who gave a befitting final farewell; she saluted her father's coffin, draped in the national flag. This was a glowing tribute to leadership at its best.

'Never give up optimism, not even when faced by stubborn and unforeseen adversities.'

—*MUKESH AMBANI*

CASE 3

'Valour, Abnegation, Sacrifice: Śaurya, Ātmasayamam, Tyāga' is the motto of the Mumbai Fire Brigade, the fire brigade serving the city of Mumbai, Maharashtra. It is responsible for the provision of fire protection as well as responding to building collapses, gas leakage, oil spillage, road and rail accidents, bird and animal rescues, fallen trees and taking appropriate action during natural disasters. Each and every officer exemplifies selfless duties and leadership.

On 2 June 2016, at 4 p.m., a major fire broke out at Metro House, which houses Cafe Mondegar, close to the Regal Cinema, at Colaba Causeway, a popular shopping district. There were about fifty fire trucks, from every station of South Mumbai, which included jumbo-tanker aerial-ladder platforms, turn-table ladders and regular fire trucks. The operation continued for almost two days, with fire tenders making refill trips. The two officers, S. Rane and M.D. Desai, were killed after the building caught fire and collapsed. They were trapped under the burning debris and could not be rescued. They were cremated at the Chandanwadi crematorium in Marine Lines. Their death was not just a matter of accident. It was a choice of sorts. M.D. Desai, had once before suffered injuries during the fire at the Mont Blanc skyscraper in Kemp's Corner in South Mumbai. Seven people had died in the incident. Memory of this sad episode did not deter this brave heart. His wife broke down in front of her husband's mortal remains as she narrated how the couple had planned the evening before M.D. Desai had left for work that day.

'The most difficult challenges turn out to be the ones you least expect.'

—*KUMAR MANGALAM BIRLA*

CASE 4

The Kargil War, also known as the Kargil conflict, was an armed conflict between India and Pakistan that took place between May and July 1999 in the Kargil district of Kashmir and elsewhere along the Line of Control (LOC). In India, the conflict is also referred to as 'Operation Vijay' (Operation Victory); the aim of the Indian operation was to clear the Kargil sector. The cause of the war was the infiltration of Pakistani soldiers and Kashmiri militants into positions on the Indian side of the LOC, which serves as the de facto border between the two states. During the initial stages of the war, Pakistan blamed the fighting entirely on independent Kashmiri insurgents, but documents left behind by casualties and later statements by Pakistan's Prime Minister and Chief of Army Staff showed involvement of Pakistani paramilitary forces, led by General Ashraf Rashid. The Indian Army, later on, supported by the Indian Air Force, recaptured a majority of the positions on the Indian side of the LOC infiltrated by the Pakistani troops and militants. With international diplomatic opposition, the Pakistani forces withdrew from the remaining Indian positions along the LOC. The war is one of the most recent examples of high-altitude warfare in mountainous terrain, which posed significant logistical problems for the combating sides.

'I'll either come back after raising the Indian flag in victory or return wrapped in it,' said leadership icon Captain Batra. On 1 June 1999, when the Kargil war was to erupt, Captain Vikram Batra's unit was sent to Kargil to recapture the Point 5140—of utmost importance to India. Point 5140 was at a height of 17,000 feet. While reaching Point 5140, the enemy commander provoked the Captain on radio, 'Why have you come here Shershah, you will not go back.' Captain Batra was the last person to back away from a fight; he replied, 'We shall see within one hour who remains at the top.' In a short while, Captain Batra and his company of troops killed eight enemy soldiers and captured a heavy anti-aircraft machine gun, neutralising the advantageous peak. Mission Point 5140 was a success. Soon after he spoke to his Commanding Officer (CO), '*Yeh dil mange more!*' (This heart desires more). The next chapter was Point 4750, where he was dared again by the enemy who said, 'Shershah, nobody shall be left to lift your dead bodies'. Shershah, as nicknamed by his CO retorted, 'Don't worry about us; pray for your safety.' Later, he re-captured Point 4750 and hoisted the national flag. His heart, in zeal of patriotism wanting victory, made him volunteer for his third task of re-capturing point 4875. On 5 July 1999, after thrashing intruders, his company and others lead by Captain. Anuj Nayyar, re-captured the peak. The enemy counter-attacked on 7 July but the team retaliated with full force. During the exchange of fire, Captain Batra's junior, Lt. Naveen was hit and Shershah jumped to his rescue. The Lt. was pleading to let him continue to which he replied, 'You are the one with kids; back away!' And while saving his comrade, a bullet found its way to Captain Batra's heart and the brave captain with the words, 'Jai Mata Di' fell on the ground to become immortal in our hearts. Indeed, such brave hearts lead by example. They never say 'go'; they say 'let's go'. They lead.

'Leverage your right-brain thinking and see the forest beyond the tree. This way larger patterns and opportunities emerge.'
—*ANAND MAHINDRA*

Bibliography

- Peter Casey, *The Greatest Company in the World?: The Story of TATA*; USA: Penguin, 2014.
- R.M. Lala, *Creation of Wealth*; India: Penguin, 2006.
- Morgen Witzel, *Tata: The Evolution of a Corporate Brand*; India: Penguin, 2010.
- R.M. Lala, *Beyond the Last Blue Mountain: A Life of J.R.D. Tata*; USA: Penguin, 1992.
- Stephen R. Covey, *The 7 Habits of Highly Effective People*; USA: Free Press, 1989.

PERFECT APPRAISAL

Performance appraisal is the process of evaluating and documenting one's performance on the job. It is part of career development. This book deals with the appraisal process, training for appraisal, pitfalls in appraisal and the dos and don'ts of appraisal.

Perfect Appraisal provides simple techniques to a perfect appraisal with a holistic approach.

PERFECT NEGOTIATION

In order to settle differences, one needs to master the skill of negotiation. Without this skill, conflicts and disagreements will arise. This book deals with the process of negotiation and its different stages: preparation, discussion, goals, win-win outcome and agreement.

Perfect Negotiation helps you master the different types of negotiation formats, styles, and preparing strategies for negotiation.

PERFECT COMMUNICATION

Communication is the process of sharing information, knowledge or meaning. What matters most is the 'response-ability'; response is more important than the message. Listeners must not just hear; they must listen. This book deals with speaking skills, writing skills and listening skills.

Perfect Communication is much more than just this.

PERFECT ASSERTIVENESS

Assertiveness is important in all forms of communication. It is a way of relating to others that respects both your own and other people's needs, wants and rights. Aggressiveness provokes counter-aggression, assertiveness doesn't. This book spells out assertiveness training, responses—passive, aggressive and assertive, effective communication, assertiveness skills and the benefits of being assertive.

Perfect Assertiveness helps you understand assertiveness as a life skill.

PERFECT MEETING

Meetings help one to build rapport. They are a forum for inter-learning and understanding; a platform to share information. *Perfect Meeting* is about the basic skills of management. This book deals with effective meetings, conference meetings, stand-up meetings, one-on-one meetings and the tasks and skills of the chairperson.

Perfect Meeting helps you generate cooperation and commitment to attain higher levels of performance.

PERFECT CV

A curriculum vitae (CV) or résumé presents a record of your qualities, skills and experience to an employer, so that your suitability for a particular job can be assessed. In Latin, 'curriculum vitae' means 'the way your life has run' and 'résumé' is the French word for 'summary'. This book deals with making a CV special, writing a CV with lack of experience, tailoring a CV and digital and online CVs.

Perfect CV helps you to compile your CV and suggests ways to improve it.

PERFECT PRESENTATION

Presentation skills are critical as they help one to inform, motivate and inspire others. It is a means to get a message across to the listeners, with a persuasive element. This book talks about the canons of persuasive presentations, verbal and non-verbal communication, styles of presentation and the opening and closing of a presentation.

Perfect Presentation helps you master the art of making effective presentations.